PLANT PARTS

Why Do Plants Have Leaves?

Celeste Bishop

PowerKiDS
press.

New York

Published in 2016 by The Rosen Publishing Group, Inc.
29 East 21st Street, New York, NY 10010

First Edition

Editor: Sarah Machajewski
Book Design: Mickey Harmon

Photo Credits: Cover (leaves) Sofiaworld/Shutterstock.com; cover, p. 1 (logo, frame) Perfect Vectors/Shutterstock.com; cover, pp. 1, 3–4, 7–8, 11–12, 15–16, 19–20, 23–24 (background) djgis/Shutterstock.com; p. 5 Romas_Photo/Shutterstock.com; p. 6 Jajaladdawan/Shutterstock.com; p. 9 Elena Elisseeva/Shutterstock.com; p. 10 photolinc/Shutterstock.com; p. 13 Tischenko Irina/Shutterstock.com; p. 14 Africa Studio/Shutterstock.com; p. 17 The Curious Travelers/Shutterstock.com; p. 18 ArTDi101/Shutterstock.com; p. 21 Nataliia Melnychuk/Shutterstock.com; p. 22 Iakov Kalinin/Shutterstock.com.

Library of Congress Cataloging-in-Publication Data

Bishop, Celeste, author.
 Why do plants have leaves? / Celeste Bishop.
    pages cm. — (Plant parts)
 Includes index.
 ISBN 978-1-5081-4221-8 (pbk.)
 ISBN 978-1-5081-4222-5 (6 pack)
 ISBN 978-1-5081-4223-2 (library binding)
 1. Leaves—Juvenile literature. I. Title.
 QK649.B57 2016
 575.5'7—dc23
                                    2015021403

Manufactured in the United States of America

CPSIA Compliance Information: Batch #BW16PK: For Further Information contact Rosen Publishing, New York, New York at 1-800-237-9932

Contents

Leaves are one of the most important plant parts. They come in many shapes and sizes.

Plants make their own food.
They use their leaves to do this.

Leaves take in sunlight and air to make food. How does this work?

Leaves have parts that make them green. These parts also take in energy from the sun.

Leaves are covered in tiny holes. The tiny holes help leaves take in air.

Air and energy from the sun mix with water inside the plant. The plant turns them into sugar. This is how it gets food.

What do leaves look like? Most leaves are flat. Some leaves are shaped like **hearts**.

pine needles

Pine needles are a kind of leaf. They don't look like leaves at all!

Some leaves change color in the fall. New leaves grow in the spring.

Plants can't live without leaves.
They need leaves to make
their food!

Words to Know

heart

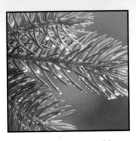

pine needles

Index

A
air, 8, 12, 15

F
food, 7, 8, 15, 23

S
sugar, 15
sun, 11, 15
sunlight, 8

Websites

Due to the changing nature of Internet links, PowerKids Press has developed an online list of websites related to the subject of this book. This site is updated regularly. Please use this link to access the list: www.powerkidslinks.com/part/leaf